If Wishes Were Horses...

Poetry with Illustrations

By

Meryl M Williams

©M Williams, 2025

ISBN: 9781917778923

The Poet Meryl M Williams b1966

Meryl originally trained in biomedical sciences then settled in Bath to write poetry and prose. Her inspiration comes from the natural world but she also enjoys walks along her local canal where the heritage architecture is just as fascinating.

Most of Meryl's writing has raised funds for local and national good causes plus she loves to undertake sponsored walks. As a survivor of mental health, she writes for well being also.

This new book contains line drawings, a technique also seen in Mortymer House - A Novella.

Other works by the same Poet and Author.

Novellas

The Judge Jones Trilogy
Judge Jones Resurgam

Mortymer House
My Lady's Sovereign

Poetry with Photographs

Moods in Bloom
A Waterfall of Words
This Firm Foundation – Contemporary Bath Abbey Life

Autobiography

Treasure Within – A Memoir

IF WISHES WERE HORSES...

Breeding, feeding, living, dying
Birds are wild and free
I wish that I was just that way
No other way to be!

But if wishes were horses
Beggars would ride, as dear old
Mother said, so here I am
Bound by your side
Until we both are dead.

For now the spring is on its way
All bulbs are bursting too
Note Magnolia comes to bud
Before the leaves come through.

Ride the storm, it's nothing new
A poet's always good and true
For here I am and there are you,
So if wishes were horses
We'd ride on to Timbuctoo!

EUROPEAN HORNBEAM

Noble, aged, fine old tree
With branches bare in March
Lichen coats many twigs
While it's bark is gnarled and dark.

When summer comes, the leaves burst forth
Then seeds like spinning feathers
In clusters of pale, pretty green
Flying high 'til they litter local paths.

A face is seen amidst those boughs
Made by one removed
While all around are bulbs in bloom
Yet too cold to tempt those leaves.

Underneath the tree, a sturdy, solid bench
While children play on slide and frame
I really do believe indeed
This tree is older than my home.

As magpies nest in Vicky's hedge
While sun or shade both come and go,
Those branches see much more than we
For endless seasons round.

Plate 1 A Hornbeam. This is in a disused graveyard near Bristol bus station.

A WELSH GIRL AT HOME

At my castle, Dunster House,
I'm warm and above all dry
The lunch I cooked was good for me
No reason then to cry.

All doldrums pass with light of day
The nights grow shorter now
I feel a rush of cheerfulness
However grim the winter sky.

Although you went, no reason why
But muse they come and go
I'm sure 'twill always be so!

The sofa has seen better days
It's faux leather pads are torn
I'll put a crochet cover o'er
To give it a whole new dawn.

Feelings of such optimistic fervour
May darken down a valley
A slough of despond known before
Yet always very shallow.

The sunshine always does return
A mood of joy will follow
So soon to be a time for tea
Then out the hills to hollow!

AUSTRALIAN CRUNCH

Well it's hard as rock
Unless you soak
The cake in chocolate sauce

It's sweet and comes
On Friday night
A weekly treat of course.

We dread to think what's in it
We often simply bin it
'Twill break our teeth, the spoon
And so forth.

Plate 2 Dunster House from Springfield Park, Bath

HILL TOP MIST

Dense, impenetrable
Moist, dank, gloom-ridden,
Sunshine all forgotten now
Fog has taken over.
Wreaths of wraiths
Over fields of furrows
Bogs of burrows
At least it's all outside
And I don't have to drive.

Blessings heaped upon my shoulder
Good food, great coffee, ice cold water
Sad songs, warm chair
Cushions to relax upon

Just the quiet need for solitude
Some peace, a pinch of privacy
A moment away from all demand
To do this thing just for me.

Tomorrow brings its own trouble
Today will now suffice
For never fret about the not yet
Or darken your brow with all things lost
In the fog of might have been.

SOMERSET LEVELS

Undulating, green like velvet,
The landscape breathes of life.

Deceptive in the May hot sun
Dryer today but flooded before.

Would they not be able to grow rice?
If water soaks this earth, I wonder.

From the levels, stark and bold,
Arises Glastonbury's Tor.

Topped by St Michael's Tower
While mists of Avalon surround at dawn.

There is a beauty here, of agriculture
Fields and form.

Then further on my travels
O'er the Mendips, back to town,
A place to call my own.

LEVEL PLAYING FIELD

I'm a child of the comprehensive system
With no complaints to make.

But quoting St Paul who writes to say
We're all in a race, the discipline is the same.

We all must train but however we begin
Only one the prestigious prize can win.

So equalling all opportunity, a very laudable aim
With all our best endeavour the results are never the same.

Frustration comes often with expectations
Beyond our earthly scope, if you want more
Disappointment may be your lot.

Contentment is a quality rarely found today
But as we keep on striving the farmer has
Mown the hay,
Scent fills the air and life goes on.

HEVER IN RED

Anne grew up in this Kent castle
Red brick with extensive grounds
Happy childhood, little dreaming
Her lot would be to wear a crown.

Henry was a monster tyrant
Knew how to have his total say
He reformed the church
Divorced his Spanish wife
But his mores were just exaggerated
Compared with the norm of his day.

Men across the world have said
If there is no son, the wife must pay
So Henry is a mere example
Of traditional values brutally made.

Much of history written by men
Shows Henry as merciless to extreme
Yes indeed, he executed many
Simply if they did not agree.

Five hundred years later
We can see, the oft repeated history
For women who fail to fit the mould
Are still derided as an abnormality.

It's said that Anne was quite ambitious
Her role at Court preferred to a Nunnery
She paid in blood as red as the brick
Of her childhood home, where visitors now make
Wonder at our bloodshot past
With this a portrait made to last.

CACOPHONY

Above the wild cacophony
The frenzied outrage, born of bass,
Sings out the songbird, sweet, clear, chaste.

Its timely treble trembles here
Upon the wind, a note of cheer
Soothing, inspiring, free of fear.

Flying high on winds of chill
Staying close or gone at will
Blackbird, blue tit, finch or lark
Heralds morning's end of dark
Greets with carols, sunshine's spark.

Oh for wings to fly with thee
Over land, hill, dale or sea
Chained to this a dry land fate
I long for your less hampered state
As your shadow follows free.

SEVEN HILLS

Bath, Rome, Edinburgh,
Not forgetting Y Fenni
A Tribute to H

He ran every year
Just plimsolls for gear with shorts
A man of iron.

A good man and true
Older than Radio wave
Almost a hundred.

Peace to run last race
Seven hills in the heavens
We wish H goodbye.

   Plate 3 A depiction of Anne Boleyn from the portrait at the Tudor exhibition, Holburne Museum,

Bath. With thanks to the National Portrait Gallery, London.

CHERRY BLOSSOM PERFECTION

Cherry blossom, fruit follows

Bees are buzzing, my honey blooms

Sweeter than any wine of desire
Your presence lights a long held fire

Dreaming of your arms held fast
Oh! Dearest will our passion last?

Tomorrow is another day
For you are always on your way

I'll be a treasured aspirant
To all we both believe and want

Maybe all these fancied flights
Are just a moment of hot air

But would you touch my heart once more
To show you really care?

It's good to know you're still alive
For with you I will always thrive
And if we both should part in time
I'll not forget that you were mine!

Plate 4 Cherry Blossom from an avenue of trees, Springfield Park, Bath.

THE RED KITE

A very distinctive bird of prey
Classified as a Raptor
See the deeply forked tail
With a brick red underbelly
Black markings and
Finger like wings.

This wondrous, enormous bird
Treated me to a fly past today,
I rushed to identify what I'd seen
But remembered there's a sanctuary
Not all that far away.

Hearkening to the turn of the Millennium
The Abergavenny Tapestry
It's said the Red Kite returned
To the hills from whence it haled.

It seemed a sign or portent
To see this Welsh bird pass
Perhaps the day is dawning
When love meets the Poet at last.

Plate 5 Artist's impression of the Red Kite.

EXOTIC BLOOMS

An orchid with bright pink blooms,
With the exotic promise of yet more buds,
Long stemmed and lovely, such waxy, green leaves
In a white, textured, ceramic pot
Cause for consideration as this amazing plant
Has come from a nursery, whilst its cousins
In the rainforest would be aghast if they knew.

Nearby, gathering dust, is a very similar plant
Made of plastic, same colour, in a shiny pot
Atop a pile of books and not needing any light.
The real orchid in the window is no doubt
Bred to last one season, the challenge here
Is to persuade it to flower once more
While its plastic friend is in bloom
Year on year.

GOLD FINCHES

Yellows, tinged with red
A sight becoming less rare
Rejoice, birds are there.

AWFUL APRIL

Looking out my window
The Radio spills out gloom
A personal, black, fluffy rain cloud
Hangs above my room.

All around are splodges of blue
Oh come back rain and fall dear,
It's time we heard from you!

The land is dry and barren
Grass withers, flowers fade
But sadly my private rain cloud
Is leaving nought but shade.

Wind comes from the West
My cloud is drifting away
I'm not in the mood
For sunshine or pleasure
I just want rain to come in ample measure.

But lo the cloud is growing
Expanding in its mass
While my local park is ruined
By diggers drilling grass

Cold the day, dark the mood
In the morning I may be paid
Well, then I'll change my mind.

FIELDS OF RAPE

Ablaze with yellow
The fields amaze my senses
Both sides of the bus

No gaps, no empty spaces
Rape grows, for fuel or food
For all of us.

So British, I buy
Oil for economy's sake
Healthy? Who's to say?
It even makes my cake!

POPULAR CULTURE

A song to lighten
Yet some are so full of woe
Dispels my sorrow.
Magpies chatter here
Nestlings cheep, no matter what
A song for all time.

Plate 6 Cloud formation with angels wings effect.

PAST, PRESENT, FUTURE

We lived, we loved, so long ago
All memory vivid lasts
A fleeting glimpse, not here but where
You live, you love, you are.

Gone the Frost series, sunshine comes
Time to sail away
Into the wide, blue yonder
Forever and a day.

I never cared for long, thin men
A shorter variety has my heart
All those chaps of softer chins
Have made me want to part.

Part with good things for all that's better
A mountain top for seaside view
Well, they cry, what's there to do?
Always patient, lovely you!

Perhaps I'll grow too old to care,
Oft' I feel you're always there
But if I never see my dream
My memory lives and you've been seen.

I saw you and I know it's true
That one day I will be with you
So take this cup of kindness thus

Place my hand unto your lips
I know I will arrive alive
The chance has come, let the sun shine.

MY MUSE AND I

Odd tasting tea
Salt in the sugar bowl
My friend leaves me to complain!

STAINED GLASS

Red, green, blue, splashes
Upon the stone cold flags there
Sun pours in dappled.

PENTAGON

My muse had drawn a pentagon
Made up of meaningful segments
Each part a point on a journey
From diagnosis to recovery

My task then was to draw
Using a desk top facility
A master plan from red to green
With every service placed in triangles.

It worked wonderfully in squares
Looked perfect in circles
But my muse was determined
And must surely have his way.

The finished art was a pie chart
Made up of wedges with circular edges
I liked it best in squares
Because text boxes have no curves.

But the finished pie chart plan
Was finally accepted by Ron
Time has since moved on
For today it's all updated

Now, one can have a pentagon
Which would have been amazing

It's possible to upgrade it
But the most important part
Was text of what's accessed
Or the master plan produced
Of a way out of winter blues.

I will always feel the pleasure
Of this task achieved and done
Then the kindness of a reward
Has my heart so surely won.

DECORATIVE TOUCH

I was eating toast
Gazing out at the City
I saw four chimneys.

Three, one after another
Were topped with silver cowls
Spiral, metal, pretty.

Looks a nice touch, there
Functional also pleasing
Keeps birds away too.

BATH DEEP LOCK

Glaring into its icy depths
On a cold, wet, autumn day
I ponder on this man made marvel
Where water is held in check
 By paddles of lock gates
Newly painted by volunteers of today.

Above the lock is found a lake
Where boats may turn or pass
For this is the point, where
Our local canal into the river pours.
A tiny footbridge, not for the nervous,
Accesses the other side
Here a swan glides safely
No thought of time or tide.

Indeed all time suspends here
On a waterway of yesteryear
Quickly a fly past by a bright bird
The blue and orange kingfisher.
Drops of rain are falling
As ducks dip, dive and so
It's time to head for home now
Make a brew and write a poem.

Plate 7 Bath Deep Lock from the road outside Widcombe High Street, Bath.

BIBLICAL RAIN

Awaking one night
Dawn slow to emerge
A thousand drops descending
Like locusts in the field

Hammering on the roof
Streaming down the walls
Ripples in the pools of moisture
Saturated grass next to wet paving stones.

Gazing from my window
Three wagtails fought for food
A single magpie chattered
So silently I prayed.

The friends I left behind me
Are never to be seen
But though the darkness blinds me
The rain makes trees more green.

So staying even longer
Than what I did intend
I'll watch the raindrops falling
Until I reach my end.

TOWN AND CORPORATION

I walked, intent on taking the bus
Passing our Council offices
Where an orderly crowd gathered.

Was it a fire alarm?
Or merely that opening hours
Were just about to start.

There, one man stood apart
Lost in thought or inner
Soliloquy

What's on his mind?
Is he just here about recycling?
Must he pay the dreaded tax?
He seems a mile from here,
Musing on the weather, perhaps.

Where is his lift home?
Is he meeting his spouse?
Well, I can only guess,
Keep walking, then board my bus!

TYTHE BARN

Pictured, a barn in Wells
Where water flows through street and gully
Built in the shape of the cross
Even down to the arrow slits
For protection in troubled times
During the fourteenth Century.

Its sister is even bigger
Residing in Bradford on Avon, Wiltshire
Those huge, wooden doors
Behind, the grain would be stored.

Supportive the flying buttress
Restored a slate, sloped roof
It's looking amazing yet elderly
So cool inside, set apart
Dignified and aloof.

In front a modern park
Where children play and sing
Behind, I cannot access
But what an extraordinary thing.
Sober to think of this relic
Of a bygone Feudal age,
When little in fact, has changed.

Plate 8 A Tythe Barn in Wells, Somerset with its porch in the North wall.

MIDPOINT VIEWPOINT

Englishcombe Lane, Bath
Bisects a hillside pretty.
A bench, halfway for sitting.

Over yonder, Beckford's Tower then
New build houses, stark at Ensleigh
Lower, the Georgian splendour
Of Fairfield Park and Camden.

In front is Moorfields Park
There, a brick with wooden structure
To house the voles, bats, beasts
With an area all of grass.

Informative the plaque
Depicting wild bee orchid
Butterflies, moths, the bees
Another bench,
What's not to love?

Sonnets of the South

(I)   Brigadoon

Lost in a timeless warp of age
The city swathed in fog today
Emerging Crescents for sun and moon
But on the hillside, a concrete
Block for Academia, Chaplaincy
And a Sports Village bright and new.
Baths for Romans, Georgians too
Take the waters to heal and soothe
Warmth to heat the Abbey floor
Come inside our open door.
Nestling under seven hills
Buildings built to last all weather
Columns curly, Doric are dull
Iambic here with ram horns full
Of ancient symbolism
Anointed with the oil of Chrism.

(II)   Plasterwork

Decorative ceilings, ornate in white
Made of horse hair, egg, to delight
Curls, leaves, grapes in abundance
With a central chandelier to light
The night of dancing, recitals
Reading aloud, pass times right
Before the dawn of video games

Smartphones, gadgets
Electricity captured in a frame
When society met with all their neighbours
Speaking face to face, accepting favours
Gentlemen paying calls with cards
Delivering posies of scented flowers
Now the roses bloom scent free
Bought online or from the grocer
Are we really any wiser?

(III)   Last Love

Salisbury, a small yet fairer city
Red brick from the local clay
I love to visit for the day
Climbing the Tower, amazing to see
A fox left by a stonemason
Who once a psychiatrist had been.
Stained glass from a modern age
Ecclesiastical blue with crucifix displayed
Cockerel crowing three times for Peter
Martyred yet holding Heaven's key.
An etching in glass of all that's true,
With a back cloth of black velvet
To articulate the light and yet
It's dark indeed now you're not here
You still remain within my core.

Sonnets of the North

(I)   Kirk Hammerton

An Anglo-Saxon Church of ageing walls
A Manse with sumptuous gardens on our walk
The wisdom of the locals, using chalk
To keep away the slugs and all that crawls
With vegetables in beds as lilies bloom
A mug to mark the year's Millennium
Henry served in Royal Navy in the War
My father's ashes rest, no turmoil now
He is at peace in this, the Vale of York
While Village Cricket plays on by the River
Flowing as it wends it's way to Cathal,
A bridge so often closed by Ouse in flood
The local pub alas it had to close.
Here, once a week, the bus comes round and drives
All folk to fetch their groceries
Then rain stops play and cricket's gone to tea!

(II)   Festival Fever

A long standing friend and I
Climbed to the top of Arthur's Seat,
An ancient site, beneath which
The Scottish Parliament meets.
 A view of Edinburgh Castle
The other end of the Royal Mile
Full of shops, "we stock your Tartan",
But of Boyce, no mention or sign!

It certainly made me smile.
Festivals have amazing appeal
Street musicians sell their poetry,
A songster with a Honky Tonk
Sings "blue moon", and "New York".
I've been back to visit St. Giles
To hear a talk to while an hour
All the Coats of Arms of patrons
In the stained glass, just like Bath Abbey
Coming away, a boat on the Forth
Under the bridge to an island of birds
A wonderful scene of natural worlds
Tinctured by man, to leave his mark.

(III)   De-Industrialisation

At South Wales, Tonteg in fact,
Cooling Towers nestled
At the foot of Power Station Hill.
I've seen them at Didcot
Collapsed on the television
Two remained at Newcastle
A wonder for my friend
Who'd not seen them before!
Removed now, a relic of a bygone era
A time when coal reigned supreme
The technology of yesteryear
Giving way to wind farms
From the Mendips to the North Sea.
Travelling North by coach
A route lined with fields all full

Of solar panels, a modern age is here!

A SPANISH SONG

I was only three
My Dad and I danced twirling
A song "Spanish Flea".

Years later, a friend
Had the same record to play
We'd listen all day!

Father liked Bolero
The grocer in my life now
Said "sing it",
So I practised in front
Of the bathroom mirror.

Music binds us closer
It's draw will never fail
One day that infamous grocer
Will hear me sing again.

JUDICIOUS PRUNING

A lovely rose, pink and surrounded
By buds with a super abundance
Of leaves in such rich, magnificent greens
After I trimmed the hips, not damaging
The tiny sprouting tips of new, leaflets emerging.

The rose bush seems happy
Beneath a shady tree
While all around, are weeds covering
The ground, that appear just instantly.

Bobbles of sticky buds
Adorn those flowers out of place
While ivy takes the tree by storm
As a white shrub shows its face.

Its an amazing, tiny wilderness
But see the extraordinary thing –
Nesting birds have visited
To clean out the food therein.

A bench is here for resting
While at its busy back
A shrub of cheery yellow
That blooms so early with
Prickly leaves of evergreen delight.

Such a feast for the eyes

In a small, communal garden
A must see every morning,
With a little wicket gate
A space for magic or mindful thriving.

Plate 9 A cultivated rose resembling a wild or dog rose with petals and sepals.

FLAMINGOES IN FASHION

These pink, enormous birds
With long necks and spindly legs
Run before they can fly
Feeding on shrimps from whence
They attain the pigment or dye.

Here they were photographed at Jersey Zoo
But they roam where're they will
At Slimbridge wildfowl trust too.

Just about six years ago
Flamingoes were all the rage
On fabrics, plastic ware and sculpture
Then no further mention was made.

Rainbows just took over
As the symbol of inclusivity
But how these fantastic birds are faring or
Where they're from remains a mystery.

Plate 10 Flamingoes at Jersey Zoo, 2001.

USE OR ORNAMENT?

Fountains play profusely,
Rising from the concrete
Despite all the warnings
Children play in the water
And parents soak their feet
A respite from city heat.

The jet force of the spurt
Could knock you off your feet
They cover a wide area
At a Piazza off the street.

I found them first in Manchester
They have them in Sheffield too
Hours of fascination, just to watch
All that water shooting through.

Higher, ever higher,
The jet streams rise and fall
From just a little bubble
To a cascading waterfall.

I found I have a photo
That I had taken there
It shot in time an image
Then in Bristol there they are.

The water ever recedes itself

Back from whence it came
And lo, it's shooting up again
Like an endless merry go round.

Well as the children play
Then grow out of this jolly day
I must return to my departure point
Coming back for another foray!

SPROUTING

Sprouting in my fridge
A rebellious garlic clove
Planted, now on the window ledge
Growing as fast as a bulb can move.
A single, green shoot; a tender, narrow blade
So strong but yet so delicate
As it widens while I give thanks today.
For from one single clove many can be made.
A trick that I've been taught
Is to crush it beneath a wide knife
Using the heel of my hand
Second nature to a crafty chef.
This miracle of life
Amazes every time,
A mindful great release
When nothing seems to rhyme!

MY ACCOMPANIST

Timothy lived a useful life
He'd achieved a music degree
A kind support of all I've done
Giving feedback so diligently.

His pursuits were wide and varied
From folk groups and the viola
To virtuosic mastery
On the descant recorder.

He had a quiet wisdom
That only those can know
Who've overcome great suffering
To rise in glory now.

We pray he's found his peace
Amongst the heavenly band
For as his life was fruitful
I respect this goodly man.

Plate 11 Fountains playing, shooting up from the

ground, at Manchester's Piccadilly.

WAVERLEY

The world's oldest
Ocean going paddle steamer
Takes tourists to Bute
Along the broad Clyde
A river deep and wide.

The engine roars, the paddles spin
Greased with carbon, steel within
A Piper greets us at the Isle
Chilly in summer, arriving in style.

I sat next to the hot chimney's funnel
Painted red, bright, while underneath
A restaurant where we had soup
Taking the steamer to Lundy, a separate trip.

She's running still today
From Brighton or Ilfracombe Bay
Steaming, chugging, trippers landing
For postage stamps, maybe a sighting
Of puffins along the rocks that way.

DISCONTENT

Poets prate of miserable lives
As if it were a virtue
They think that melancholy
Makes one somehow holy.

Like the snow in March
Descending then dissolving
In a day it's gone
No sense in dwelling on.

For the news is always gloomy
We thrive upon its grit
Let's find the blessed off switch
For there's no end to it.

See the snowdrop survive
All hardy in the frost
It's thriving midst the dying
We need to get a grip.

My window shines for me
I look out on a tree
I placed a vase of flowers
For everyone to see.

Index of first lines.

A long standing friend and I.	Page 44
A lovely rose, pink and surrounded.	47
A song to lighten.	27
A very distinctive bird of prey.	21
An Anglo-Saxon church of ageing walls.	44
An orchid with bright pink blooms.	23
At my castle, Dunster House.	8
At South Wales, Tonteg in fact.	45
Ablaze with yellow.	26
Above the wild cacophony.	16
Anne grew up in this Kent castle.	14
Awaking one night.	37
Bath, Rome, Edinburgh.	17
Breeding, feeding, living, dying.	5
Cherry blossom, fruit follows.	19
Decorative ceilings, ornate in white.	42
Dense, impenetrable.	11
Englishcombe Lane, Bath.	41
Fountains play profusely.	52
Glaring into its icy depths.	35
I'm a child of the comprehensive system.	13
I walked, intent on taking the bus.	38
I was eating toast.	34
I was only three.	46
Looking out my window.	25
Lost in a timeless warp of age.	42
My muse had drawn a pentagon.	32
Noble, aged, fine old tree.	6
Odd tasting tea.	31

Pictured, a barn in Wells.	39
Poets prate of miserable lives.	58
Red, green, blue splashes.	31
Salisbury, a small yet fairer city.	43
Sprouting in my fridge.	54
The world's oldest.	57
These pink, enormous birds.	50
Timothy lived a useful life.	55
Undulating, green like velvet.	12
We lived, we loved, so long ago.	29
Well it's hard as rock.	9
Yellows, tinged with red.	24

www.ingramcontent.com/pod-product-compliance
Lightning Source LLC
Chambersburg PA
CBHW052119070526
44584CB00017B/2551